QUAKER QUICKS

Telling the Truth about God

Quaker Quicks is a new series from Christian Alternative focusing upon aspects of Quaker faith and theology. Beginning with *Quaker Roots and Branches* the series will build into a valuable resource both for Quakers and those interested in this unique expression of belief, practice and theology. Watch out for upcoming titles on Quaker theology, faith and practice, and studies in social aspects such as economics and pacifism.

Current other titles...

Quaker Roots and Branches - John Lampen
What do Quakers believe - Geoffrey Durham

QUAKER QUICKS

Telling the Truth about God

Rhiannon Grant

CHRISTIAN
ALTERNATIVE

Winchester, UK
Washington, USA

First published by Christian Alternative Books, 2019
Christian Alternative Books is an imprint of John Hunt Publishing Ltd.,
No. 3 East St., Alresford, Hampshire SO24 9EE, UK
office1@jhpbooks.net
www.johnhuntpublishing.com
www.christian-alternative.com

For distributor details and how to order please visit the 'Ordering' section on our website.

Text copyright: Rhiannon Grant 2018

ISBN: 978 1 78904 081 4
978 1 78904 082 1 (ebook)
Library of Congress Control Number: 2018938213

A CIP catalogue record for this book is available from the British Library.

Design: Stuart Davies

Printed and bound by CPI Group (UK) Ltd, Croydon, CR0 4YY, UK
US: Printed and bound by Edwards Brothers Malloy 15200 NBN Way #B, Blue Ridge Summit,
PA 17214, USA

We operate a distinctive and ethical publishing philosophy in
all areas of our business, from our global network of authors to
production and worldwide distribution.

Contents

Don't think, but look! – Ludwig Wittgenstein

For the Friend who told me how to dedicate my first book. It didn't turn out the way either of us expected, but you believed there would be one.

Acknowledgements

My heartfelt thanks to all those who have supported, engaged with, and sometimes endured my passion for talking about how Quakers talk about God. I owe particular thanks to all those who have participated in my 'Or Whatever You Call It' workshops – some anonymised insights from you appear directly in this book.

I would also like to thank Rachel Muers, whose contributions to this work have been immeasurable since before I began it; to Mikel Burley, without whom the original research wouldn't have been the same; to the University of Leeds, which funded the initial work; to Ben Pink Dandelion and Betty Hagglund of the Centre for Research in Quaker Studies, where the Gerald Hodgett Award enabled me to start taking this to a wider audience; and to Ben Wood and Janet Scott who have taught alongside me. I have also benefited greatly from the friendship of Alex Bell, Martel Reynolds, Stephanie Grant, Jim Grant, Peter Grant, and others who have discussed these and many other philosophical questions over the years.

Finally, I want to thank my Quaker communities: Watford Meeting, Beeston Meeting, Nottingham Quaker Quest Core Team, Carlton Hill Meeting (especially those who participated in my meeting for clearness), Quakers in Yorkshire, Bournville Meeting, Britain Yearly Meeting, and the Book of Discipline Revision Preparation Group.

Introduction for non-Quakers

Dear reader,

Thank you for opening this book. I hope that whatever your religious background or beliefs, reading this book will help you to think through what you know and don't know about God. Telling the truth, about God and other matters, should concern everyone. In the course of my own theological education I have learnt a great deal from religious traditions outside my own, and I would be very happy if this book was able in some small way to repay that.

Because this book draws heavily on conversations which have happened and are happening within the British Quaker community, I need to fill you in on some background by telling you some things about Quakers in general. If you are already familiar with Quaker history and practices, you may be able to skip this section and get on with the rest of the book.

A few things first about how Quakers worship. We can worship anywhere, but typically get together in a meeting house, community centre, someone's living room, or a protest site. We can worship at any time, but typically meet on Sunday mornings, a weekday evening or lunchtime, or whenever international arms deals are going down. We don't have any rituals, but we begin worship when the first person sits down and continue until some designated people shake hands at the end. We don't ordain anyone, but we do ask people to take on specific responsibilities in the community for a limited period of time. In the liberal Quaker tradition, the worship is made up of silent waiting and listening until someone is moved to speak. There's no plan. Usually there are a few words; sometimes someone sings a song; very occasionally, someone is led to be a bit more dramatic.

Worldwide, liberal or unprogrammed Quakers – silent

worship, no paid pastors – are in the minority. If you're looking for them, the United States of America and Europe are the main places, although a few can be found almost everywhere in the world. On the other hand, programmed meetings, often called Friends Churches, are common in the United States of America and some other places, especially Bolivia and Kenya. A programmed meeting typically includes biblical readings, hymns, and a talk. In this book, when I say Quakers, I am talking about liberal Quakers. This is because my research about Quakers and my experience of Quakers are all focussed on British Quakers, or to give us our formal name, the Religious Society of Friends (Quakers) in Britain. Among ourselves, we use also use the word *Friend* to address each other. Almost all British Quakers are liberal Quakers. I'm sorry I can't include a wider picture.

Quakers have managed to reach so much of the world because they started a while ago. It's traditional to date the beginning of the Quaker movement to 1652, when George Fox climbed Pendle Hill, in the north of England, and had a vision of a people to be gathered. Britain was in turmoil and many small religious groups were forming, gaining and losing followers, and often being persecuted by those in power. Fox – and other early leaders, including James Naylor and Margaret Fell – created a movement which rejected the rituals of the church, encouraged people to own their beliefs rather than relying on others, and was very popular at a time of great unrest. From the north of England, early Quakers travelled the known world, and were involved in international projects like the founding of Pennsylvania.

Over the centuries, Quaker practices have changed. Some Quakers have moved towards more typically Christian positions, continuing to hold the Bible as a core part of their faith, while other Quakers – like those I'll be discussing in this book – have focussed on experience and inspiration over texts. On the other hand, Quakers are still not afraid to take positions which put

2

them at odds with the rest of the world, and even get them arrested.

It is some of these positions – the expressions of faith in the world, or testimony – for which Quakers are best known. For example, Quakers are pacifist and Quakers see all people as equal. This has led some Quakers to take relatively controversial stances: opposing war and slavery, and supporting same-sex marriage, have all got Quakers into hot water at various times. Some Quakers are reading this and thinking: but we're not all pacifists, and we don't all support same-sex marriage. I mention this to you, non-Quaker reader, only so that you will know to take everything which follows with a suitable pinch of salt.

This is the merest scratch on the surface of Quaker history, theology, and activism. I hope it'll be enough for you to follow what I'm talking about in the rest of this book – I try and explain technical terms and the current situation as I go along – and that if you want to know more you'll consult some of the sources suggested in 'After reading this book'.

Introduction for Quakers

Dear Friend,

Thank you for opening this book. I hope that as well as describing some of the discussions our community is already having, it will be able to make a small contribution to them. If, when you've read it, you feel that you are better able to tell the truth about God as you understand it, I hope that you will share that insight (and perhaps this book!) with whatever Quaker communities you belong to.

Before I begin, I need to tell you some things about what this book does and does not aim to do. Quakers sometimes try and assign me to a 'side' in a 'debate' – but although I certainly have opinions, I don't think the terms in which current discussions are framed are very helpful. For example, I am neither a nontheist nor a 'theist'. I am not a Christian but nor do I want to see Christianity removed from the Quaker tradition. That being so, this book advocates a process of trying to get closer to the truth – something which I think is already implicit but unacknowledged in much Quaker conversation about theology – and not a specific theological position.

My beliefs about God have changed over the years, sometimes frequently. When I was a philosophy undergraduate, I used to count it a boring week if I hadn't changed my mind about something significant at least once. That means that I can think of times when I have been a Christian believer (never born-again, but willing to experiment with the whole Jesus thing), times when I have been a Goddess-worshipping neo-Pagan (I still enjoy a good Druid ritual), and times when I have been an atheist. I once read Spinoza, and decided I agreed with him, and then read a paper which argued so convincingly that he was an atheist that I saw that I was an atheist too. And then I went to meeting for worship anyway, because I was also still a Quaker.

This makes it hard for me to claim with confidence any particular label, especially in writing. I might be something else tomorrow. It also makes it hard for me to accept any proposal that Quakers should put a theological boundary on our community. Even the merest, softest touches of suggestion that in order to be a Proper Quaker one ought to believe in or be open to or accept the possibility of this or that sets me imagining ways in which I might find myself outside that boundary.

It also means that I have at some point held or tried to hold just about every faith position I describe in this book – not actually a very wide range, in world terms, since all of them are Quaker positions. Some of them I find much harder than others, but the effort itself can be rewarding. It's a kind of yoga for the soul. I hope that this book describes everything sympathetically enough that you'll be able to try it too, if you wish.

Finally, sometimes Quakers tell me that we don't do theology. I disagree, and I hope you'll keep reading for long enough for me to explain why.

What does 'doing theology' involve?

'Theology' sounds posh, doesn't it? Technical. Learned. When I was choosing subjects to study at university people advised in favour of things which ended with 'ology' and against things which ended with 'studies'. (I never did get a clear ruling on 'osophy', but went ahead with a degree in Theology and Philosophy anyway.) This is pure bias, but it's important to begin by being aware of the prejudices which exist in our culture. One of the roots of this bias is the favouring of technical words, especially those from Greek and Latin, over 'plainer', English words. Because of this, it's also traditional to start a discussion of a question like 'what is theology?' by informing the reader that it's formed from two Greek roots, *theo* for God and *ology* for talking about things.

I can't help feeling that this is not a terribly helpful move. For one thing, knowing the root of a word doesn't tell you what it means now or all the possibilities it can encompass ('television' is from 'tele', far, and 'vision', to see, but if you'd never watched television before I don't think this would help you make sense of a Tom and Jerry cartoon). For another thing, it assumes that you know what the elements mean – and since 'what is God like?' is a key theological question, starting out by assuming even that God is a thing which can be talked about seems like a presumption.

I prefer to think of theology as existing in two streams. There's formal theology – including academic work and writing by acknowledged religious leaders – and ordinary theology, which is something people do on a daily basis. This book is primarily about the second kind, although in places I'll draw on the formal tradition as well. I learned the phrase 'ordinary theology' from Jeff Astley, who has explored how people do theology, even people who think that they don't do theology.

He gives lots of examples, but one which sticks in my mind as illustrating an ordinary moment at which theology is clearly required is the time when you – I, everyone – has to respond to bereavement. It's easiest to focus on your response when the bereavement is at a small remove – perhaps the death was of a friend of a friend, so that you aren't grieving yourself but your friend is. How you respond, especially what you say to your friend, will depend on lots of factors, but in deciding what to say you are doing theology. Will you say that the deceased is with God now, or free from suffering, or still with your friend in their heart, or wouldn't want them to be sad? Here, as in many other places, theology is not a fully-formed system, but an off-the-cuff process in which our cultural norms, religious background, ideas about the nature of the world, and emotional intelligence come together as we strive to say something both comforting and true. Quaker theology as discussed in this book will look much more like this than like the twelve-volume academic study which is standard in some parts of systematic theology.

Just to be clear, this does not mean that Quakers do not have any formal theology. There's less emphasis on formal theology than there would be in some other religious communities, but there are Quaker theologians with formal training and official statements of Quaker theology – not always recognised as such, but they can be embedded in documents such as minutes and epistles. However, ordinary theology is much more typical of the Quaker community. Perhaps in recording some of my observations about ordinary theology in this book I formalise them, but I hope this doesn't change them beyond recognition.

Doing theology, then, is an ongoing process in which a community of people reflect on their experiences, improvise ways to articulate their ideas and experiment with different approaches to understanding the world. In Quaker thought, it's important that this process begins with experience. This doesn't exactly equate to the empirical testing of the sciences, but it has the same drive: to check that ideas are true by matching them against observations. Spiritual experiences are hard to quantify and share, so personal experience – and consequently, accounts of personal experience – becomes very important to Quaker theology. One of the things that makes this book a Quaker book, rather than an exercise in formal theology, is that I will draw on my own experience as well as quoting from other people's accounts of their experiences in working through theological ideas.

Describing experiences is a process intimately bound up with having experiences. The language which is available may shape the experiences that are possible – and it certainly shapes the ways in which they can be communicated to others. (If you're not sure about this claim, consider these questions: Could someone who had never heard of Mary, mother of Jesus, have a vision of her? If they did, could they describe it as such, or would they use words or names from their existing religious vocabulary?) From the experience and the description of it, the process of doing theology then addresses the resulting questions. These might include issues such as the origin or cause of the experience, whether it has a message or meaning for us, and how it relates to other parts of life. Answers to all of these can be shaped by, or reveal, the understanding of God which is in use.

The title of this book, 'Telling the Truth about God', is intended to reflect all these aspects of ordinary theology. It is an ongoing process – 'telling', not 'we have been told' or 'I will tell you'. It is about trying to get things right – about truth, even when that is difficult to achieve. And it has something or other to do with God, although finding out what kind of God is involved is part of the process.

Overview of this book

How do Quakers tell the truth about God? This book explores this key theological process through fourteen short chapters. My overall idea is that as Quakers, we say that we know some things, but not very much, about God, and that we are in a constant process of trying to improve our ways of saying what we do know.

I start by looking at how we know anything, and in particular I talk about the importance of experience in Quaker thought. This will be the foundation of the rest of the book, which puts personal experience – and all the complexity that brings – front and centre. The next chapter deals with an idea which follows on directly from this: that everyone has the potential to have direct access to whatever God is. Everyone's personal experience is equally important, and we do not need any specially-trained individual or magical process to stand between us and the Divine.

Having got these basics in place, I look at one way in which a group can try and get closer to the truth: through denying something which is honest but not correct. Having shown how this might be applied in the Quaker situation, I explore in more detail what happens when we refuse a particular word.

This leads me into thinking about three ways in which Quakers can respond to this situation. I look at how and why we view listening as an action, not something passive. This includes thinking about the idea that we can listen to what is behind or beyond the words someone uses. I then introduce a second response, the idea that what matters is telling our stories. Stories will be a major theme in the rest of the book. The third response I explore is the ways in which Quakers might find or create new words.

Looking at how Quakers create new ways of speaking, I

describe one which is becoming increasing common: the list of words for God. I give examples of this pattern and talk about what the advantages and disadvantages might be, as well as asking what assumptions it involves.

In the next few chapters, I look at some specific groups of words which appear in the lists and how these relate to other discussions which are happening among Quakers. I explore issues around Christianity and Quakerism by looking at the understandings of Jesus which show up when people think about the words they use for God. I also explore how Quakerism comes into new relationships with other religious traditions, using Buddhism as an example, and how Quakers can respond to new ideas by looking at the use of masculine and feminine words for the Divine.

Three chapters of the book then return to the important themes which were introduced early on. Experience is very important to Quakers and I return to this to say more about how issues around religious language can also be very personal ones. The process of denial appears again in a chapter which explores not believing in God (a position often called 'nontheism' in the Quaker community) and understandings of 'God' which do not include many, if any, of the things God is traditionally said to be. I also return to the practice of looking at what Quakers actually say to consider the well-loved phrase 'that of God in everyone'. I suggest that this includes a focus on people which allows plenty of space for disagreement about other aspects of God's nature.

Finally, I ask where all this leaves us as Quakers. I conclude that the process of telling the truth about God – theologising – needs to be an ongoing one. I also say that it is not something which takes us away from other aspects of Quaker work, such as prayer or activism. It is already involved in both.

Experience first: how Quakers know things

There is a view, sometimes jokingly labelled the militant agnostic view, that we cannot know anything about God at all. If God were to exist in any way, this position says, that God would be so unknowable, so different to us and so unreachable, that we couldn't be said to know anything about God anyway. A view like this is a fairly good fit for some aspects of Quaker thought. In unprogrammed worship there's no apparent need to make a knowledge claim – certainly, no specific claim to know anything is required on a particular occasion – and a refusal to have a creed could be seen as a refusal to claim to know anything. The position also seems to get right something about the unknowability and what theologians call the ineffability of God: our inability to express the truth about God in words.

However, where the 'militant agnostic' view falls down for the Quaker community is that some Quakers do claim to know things about God. In particular, a lot of Quakers focus on their spiritual experience. This can take lots of forms. These range from the kind of 'peak experience' in which someone is briefly but completely enveloped in a feeling such as connection, oneness with the Divine, joy, or enlightenment, to subtle, background experiences such as a shift of mood. Sometimes people report these experiences as a consistent long-term sense of happiness or compassion, or moments which are 'touched by angels' when something which happens in a relationship between people is also understood as a contact with God. All these and many other experiences can be understood in Quaker terms as the movement of the Spirit.

What someone claims to know on the basis of their experience will depend on both the nature of that experience and the framework within which they interpret it. For example, someone who has experienced a 'leading', in which they felt that the Light showed them a way forward in a difficult situation or the Spirit made it possible for them to be in the right place at the right time, may make strong claims about the will of God and what God wants them to do, or – if their understanding of God is of a less personal being which does not have desires or a will – focus on the idea that these events went with the grain of the universe, or tapped into a flow of energy through the world which does not have a conscious goal but is moving towards something positive such as peace or love.

Is this enough to be convincing? It's possible that these people are making a mistake about their experience. Apparently spiritual experiences might be like dreams or mirages – tricks of the mind or the light which make someone think that they have had a spiritual experience when there's actually another explanation. Even if spiritual experiences do arise from something we can call 'God', there's enough disagreement about what that source is like that there's plenty of room for doubt. Even someone who has a vision of Jesus doesn't automatically come away from that experience with a clear belief in a personal Christian deity, so the connection between experience and belief isn't straightforward.

An approach Quakers can try and take to this problem is to bring together a weight of evidence – building a body of collective knowledge through our corporate worship and shared experiences. This works to a certain extent. The Quaker way of making decisions, through a listening process often described as looking for the will of God for the group, gives a basis for a shared understanding of what kind of God might be involved. That isn't automatically anything which is named 'God' or would be recognised as the God of another tradition. The Nontheist Friends Network use Quaker business method for their decision making and they are clear that they see the 'will of God' as metaphorical language to explain a complex, but not supernatural, phenomenon. There are still things we can say about the Spirit which guides a Quaker meeting for worship for business, though. It can be sensed in a room. It can have a direction and make distinctions: yes this, not that. It is worth trusting.

These are pretty small knowledge claims, compared to those some religious groups would make about God. 'It can be sensed in a room' is minor compared to 'God transcends the universe' and 'it is worth trusting' stops short of 'the Divine is perfect and ultimately good'. On the other hand, they are fairly substantial knowledge claims compared with those the truly militant agnostic would have us make: 'it can help us make decisions' is a lot stronger than 'we know nothing'.

I am being cautious here. Some Quakers have faith in much more knowledge – drawing on the wisdom of Christian history, the lessons of other religious traditions, and their own experience. My own spiritual experience points to a much richer consciousness present in the world, entirely natural but beyond myself. The point of this chapter is not to try and support the biggest claim possible, but to establish that collectively, even with all our doubts kept and valued, Quakers can say that we know some small things about the Mystery often known as 'God'.

No hireling priests, or, plugging in directly

A cornerstone for all Quaker theologising is the Meeting for Worship. In the last chapter, I talked about the centrality of shared experience, and used Quaker business method as my example, but there are more general things to say about the process of meeting for worship itself.

What is meeting for worship? It is a meeting, in that it involves a group of people coming together, although it's not like typical meetings in the world of work or politics. It is not worship of something in the sense of bowing down and grovelling to an external power – although belief in an external power and submission to a divine will can be part of the process. It is not planned, as captured by the term 'unprogrammed worship'. It usually involves a lot of silence, but speech isn't completely banned and some noises (the radiators, a child burbling, birdsong) are deemed not to disturb it. Within the group who are gathered, there are typically some who have particular responsibility for the holding and quality of meeting for worship – but unless you are very well acquainted with that group, you probably can't identify them at a glance. Nobody specific is in charge, unless you include God, and there definitely isn't a priest or minister or anyone who *has* to be there or do something in order to make it work.

More importantly, meeting for worship is a process in which people, as part of a community, try to link up with whatever Higher Power, God, or Force they sense. It's not the only process which can do this – for most people, meeting for worship is one part of a wider process which can involve your whole life – but it's a time which is explicitly set aside to unite or commune with the Mystery. Quakers reject any idea of a need for mediation by a person between the individual and God. They vary a bit on whether there might be another spiritual force involved. For example, sometimes it sounds like the Spirit connects people with God; sometimes it sounds like the Spirit *is* God, and sometimes it sounds like God is so intimately present within the human being – and perhaps nowhere else – that there isn't any space between them for an intermediary to fit in.

This begins with a rejection. Early Quakers rejected the need for a priest to stand between worshippers and God, and also the need for someone learned to stand between readers of the Bible and God. They read the Bible for themselves, as part of the first generation to be able to do so regularly and easily in English, and understood their experience of the Spirit inspiring their reading as part of the same process by which the Spirit had inspired the original authors to write the biblical texts. They gathered in worship in silence or with directly inspired speech, rejecting pre-planned liturgy and outward sacraments, such as the use of water for baptism and bread and wine for communion. Quakers today return to these themes for inspiration.

Where does this rejection go? The initial results are obvious: rejecting priests, you reject their authority. (But to hold a community together, sometimes you have to appoint people to get things done – modern Quakers usually ask members of the community to spend a set period of time in a role to look after something, whether that's spiritual matters, pastoral care, decision making processes, finding people to do jobs, keeping the accounts, and other stuff that needs doing.) By rejecting the need for learning and ordination, you make all believers equal before God. (Even though some of them know more than others – for a long time, the tradition of 'recorded ministers', people who were recognised as giving helpful spoken ministry, acknowledged this.) By rejecting any intermediaries, you need to get on and do it yourself – in community if not as an individual.

Further down the road, though, there are other results of this rejection which may be less obvious at first glance. If there's no need for a priest to let people access the Spirit of Christ, is there any need for people to know about Christ in order to access God? I'll be coming back to the question about Jesus Christ specifically in the next chapter, so for now I'll focus on the question of access. If there's no need for an intermediary, is there any need to stick with the interpretations and teachings of previous generations, or should the inspiration of the Spirit as it is experienced be the only guide? Here's a place where liberal Quakers differ from some other branches of Quakerism who place much more emphasis on the Bible. Experience of the movement of the Spirit – often elided to 'spiritual experience' or just 'our experience' – is core for liberal Quakers and the rejection of anyone who stands between the person and the divine sometimes seems to extend to the Gospel writers themselves.

A factor in the development of this position is the awareness, developing from the late nineteenth century, that the authors and editors of the biblical texts were completely human. It's now clear that a close analysis using historical critical methods can show how the biblical writers brought together collections of stories from many sources, retold things to suit their audiences and purposes, chose which bits to include in the canon and left other parts out, and can generally explain contradictions and paradoxes present in the Bible through reference to human error or manipulation rather than the complexity of God's teaching. This hasn't entirely put Quakers as a community off from using the Bible as a source of inspiration and guidance. Usually there's a mix: in a typical Quaker meeting I would expect to find some people who know the Bible well and use it, some people who know it well and reject it, and a lot of people who know and either use or reject a few famous or favourite bits, while ignoring all the rest through a mixture of ignorance and a feeling of irrelevance.

From the rejection of the need for an intermediary and the drift away from the Bible, then, we get a focus on the importance of personal experience. This might be understood in a variety of ways – as the inspiration of the Spirit (coming in from outside), as the promptings of love and truth in the heart (arising from within), or as the movement of that of God within (which creates a connection between the inner and the outer). Nothing about it specifies that it must have particular conceptual elements. The Quaker understanding of the priesthood of all believers is no longer limited to those who are Christian believers, but can be extended to others who seem to have similar patterns – and then to those whose patterns of belief and religious practice are much less similar. I mention practice here as well as belief because one of the first places Quakers seem easily able to find truth outside the Christian tradition is in Buddhism. This doesn't seem to be so much about the teachings of a particular school of Buddhism (indeed, some Buddhist teachings about topics like cosmology are deeply alien to Quaker ways of thinking), but about the similarities of the practices of silent waiting in meeting for worship and silent meditation. Buddhism as presented in the West often also has a focus on methods for meditation and the importance of individuals practising regularly which, while not always sitting easily with the idea of the teacher as present in some forms of Buddhism, can sit comfortably alongside the Quaker rejection of intermediaries.

Another less expected, and some might say less helpful, implication of the rejection of intermediaries is that it can result in a focus on the individual at the expense of the community. If you don't need anyone else to help you have direct contact with God, you might not need anyone else in your religious life at all. This is not actually a position Quakers have historically taken, and a few words about why that is, and what Quakers say instead, will help to explain why it's also important to Quakers to talk to one another about God. If religion was really completely private, down to the individual alone, it wouldn't matter in the slightest if everyone believed something different.

Instead, Quakers actually rest a lot of authority in the group.

We are not, as Ben Pink Dandelion said in his Swarthmore lecture, a 'Do It Yourself' religion, but a 'Do It Ourselves' religion. Although no *special* person or object is needed to access divine wisdom, Quakers also admit the possibility that any individual might be mistaken – perhaps led astray by their personal desires. It's the group, not just the individual, which seeks to find the will of God. The most obvious situation in which Quakers use this is our decision-making procedure. We call this the 'Meeting for Worship for Business', the method by which the community gathers to listen to one another and to the Divine in order to answer specific questions – everything from 'shall we donate to such-and-such a charity?' to 'should Quakers as a group support a change in the law about assisted dying?' In this process, which tries to find the way forward which is right for the community rather than a consensus or a compromise, there are no intermediaries but also no leaders: no one person is taken to have a better connection to the Divine than another.

It is in the context of this community emphasis, in which personal experience and community participation are both important, that I am considering the question of telling the truth about God. If the emphasis swung a long way towards personal experience, everyone could just shrug and say that other people's experiences don't matter – it's *my* experiences which are important to me. If the emphasis swung the other way, completely towards the community and away from personal experience, people's different understandings of God could again be ignored in favour of whatever position the group decided to hold. Holding both together, however, demands a more complex negotiation.

A spiral of denials

How does the Quaker community try to get closer to telling the truth about God? I have already mentioned the importance of beginning with experience, which grounds some positive claims. These have the underlying structure: I know this, because I have had an experience which demonstrated it. However, in trying to move out from there into more general claims, that isn't enough – for one thing, other people have little or no reason to believe in God based on one person's experience. More importantly, the 'this' which is known through direct experience is acknowledged to be only part of the picture. There's an old joke about generalisation, which involves an astronomer, a physicist, and a mathematician on a train from London to Edinburgh. They've just crossed the border into Scotland when they pass a black sheep. 'That's interesting,' the astronomer says. 'Sheep in Scotland are black.'

'Well, some sheep in Scotland are black,' replies the physicist.

The mathematician shakes her head. 'At least half of at least one sheep in Scotland is black.'

Like these observers on a train, someone having a spiritual experience is – Quakers take it – only experiencing part of the complex truth of the Divine. Also like these observers on the train, Quakers can proceed by trying to get closer to the truth, to gradually be less wrong, by denying or correcting what has come before. In many of the discussions about the nature of God which I will be describing in this book, there is a pattern of a spiral of denials. I'll try and draw out the details as I address each case, but in this chapter I want to look at how the pattern works. I got this idea from something Rachel Muers said in a book called *God, Words and Us*.

'Consider it possible you may be mistaken,' says a frequently quoted passage in Britain Yearly Meeting's *Advices & Queries*, a core Quaker document which is read aloud regularly in meetings for worship. Considering it possible that you may be mistaken is a good idea which can cut two ways. The reader can apply it to themselves: I consider it possible that I may be mistaken. Ideally, this leads to honesty and humility, although it sometimes also leads to a pretence of humility or a misplaced tentativeness. The reader can also apply it to others: I consider it possible that she or he is mistaken. The word 'mistaken' here is an important inflection: there is no accusation of lying or wilful ignorance, just a mistake. Taken together, these two approaches can create a theological space in which people are both willing to revise their own ideas as new insights and new experiences shape them, and to challenge other people's ideas and ask questions about what makes sense and the limits of what can be known. (I say that they *can* create this space. I have known it to happen. I couldn't honestly describe it as a very common thing among British Quakers – unfortunately!)

Quakers are also frequently counter-cultural. Perhaps they are not as counter-cultural as would be desirable, from some perspectives, but along with ethical stances like pacifism in a militaristic society, any form of religiosity in a generally secular society can be seen as counter-cultural. This means that in the second move, when a Quaker considers whether or not someone else is mistaken, the 'someone else' may not be a Quaker – rather, the move is often used as part of a process of distinguishing Quakers from the surrounding culture. That's an important process for any community ('what makes us different?'). Theology isn't the only arena for this – Quakers no longer dress or speak distinctively but might point to practices like attending meeting for worship or values such as treating everyone equally – but it is a significant one, and a core part of it involves denying things which others might believe or expect Quakers to believe.

It's sometimes put as a complaint: if you ask a Quaker what Quakers believe, they often begin by telling you what they *don't* believe. I'm arguing, though, that this is a key philosophical move in Quaker theology – the denial as a step closer to truth. This doesn't mean that Quakers have yet reached the answer, and it doesn't always mean that Quakers can say yes to the opposite of the thing they're denying. Here's an example. Some churches say that the Bible is the ultimate authority. Quakers (at least liberal Quakers today) don't agree. For many, that's because their highest source of authority is experience – although some would identify something else, such as the Spirit, perhaps acting through experience, as the authority. Only some Quakers would agree with the extreme opposite, though, saying that the Bible has no authority whatsoever. Rather, the denial of *ultimate* authority to the Bible leads to a position in which Quakers can have a range of attitudes to it: reading it through their experience, with the help of the Spirit, in the light of modern critical methods, as entirely poetic, or as something they reject entirely.

In speaking to a non-Quaker, it's almost impossible to share the Quaker view of the Bible coherently without beginning by denying someone else's view. I began my example by denying a view which some churches take, but if I were asked about Quaker views of the Bible by someone I knew regarded it as irrelevant nonsense, I would also have to begin by denying that view – even though there are Quakers who do take positions something like both of those views. In speaking to other Quakers, discussion can be advanced by denying the denial of a view. In the case of approaches to biblical authority, for example, having established that a Quaker group all deny both the complete granting of authority and the denial of all relevance, we might proceed by testing whether everyone can deny a feminist assertion that the text is irretrievably sexist or examining specific passages about which we can affirm or deny a claim about authority.

The idea that I am advancing here, that a process of repeated denials can move closer to truth, seems more plausible if you are already operating – as I am – from within a Quaker framework which expects that silence is the answer to many questions and that what we can confidently know about God will be composed of more negative statements (more apophatic theology, to use the technical term) than positive statements. If you expect truths about God to be mainly positive statements, it doesn't seem like a very likely start, although by the end of this book I am aiming to show that Quakers do reach some very modest positive results. It's also, I'm aware, a determinedly optimistic assessment of the situation. Many people dislike this process of disagreeing with one another – even among the best of friends, it can feel like conflict, and any feeling of insecurity can make it seem unbearable within a community. Furthermore, since I consider it possible that I may be mistaken, it might be that I have missed the mark and whatever Quaker theology ever existed is now disappearing into a slurry of negativity. I hope that the discussion of further examples in the rest of this book will convince you otherwise.

I wouldn't say that

One form of denial is the rejection of particular words. Among Quakers, this might mean that someone rejects words which they find no longer fit their image of God: for example, a Quaker who was raised in a traditional Christian church but never connected with the idea of Jesus as a spiritual being rather than a wholly human teacher might reject the word 'Christ' because it symbolises for them what they reject from their childhood religion. For others, it might involve rejecting a whole class of words or words which seem to make a presupposition with which the individual does not agree. Some Quakers reject the word 'Creator' because they see it as opposing their understanding of evolution. Others reject all words for God which suggest that God is masculine: Father, Son, and Lord are all out. Some extend this to all gendered terms, rejecting Mother and Goddess as well, while others refuse to use any terms which suggest that God has a personal aspect – so that Parent is out, too.

In silence, it is possible to hold rejections of this kind and stop there. It may not even result in a problematic individualism as we all reject different words so long as the community is united in the practice of unprogrammed worship. However, unprogrammed worship sometimes calls for the use of words – and discussion groups, leaflet writing, and outreach almost always require them.

I have heard from some Quakers real fears about this situation. There are those who are afraid to use the words which they prefer because someone else in their meeting has rejected those terms. There are also those who worry that this method of denial leaves us without any words we can share. And – sometimes embodied by the same individual – there are also those who have strong and genuine negative emotional reactions to hearing some words for God, especially ones which they have struggled with and rejected. All these are real, understandable feelings which need to be acknowledged and validated in our communities.

Having accepted that this is the situation, how can Quakers respond? In my observations there are three responses which seem to lead to positive outcomes: attention to the interaction between speaker and hearer, story-telling and getting to know one another, and creative shaping of new ways of speaking. Let me run through these one at a time.

Listening as an action

There's a well-known Quaker story, set in North America during the time when it is being colonised, about a meeting between Quakers, some Moravians, and some Native Americans. The group have a meeting for worship, during which there's spoken ministry given in English, a language the local population don't speak. Afterwards, one of the natives says through his translator that ministry doesn't need translating, because he loves to listen to where words come from. This story was reported by John Woolman, a fact many tellers of the tale remember, and the memorable phrase is attributed to Papunehang, a fact most forget. You can draw your own conclusions about possible racist attitudes embedded in the origins and use of this story. Besides expressing an approach to Native American communities, this tale is also used to express an approach to spoken ministry (that is, the things which people are led to say into the silence during meeting for worship). In particular, it can be used to suggest that those who hear spoken ministry should let go of particular words – or even the language – and hear in it something deeper.

This idea about spoken ministry breaks with normal conversational rules, though. It's usual to try and communicate. This involves the speaker as well as the listener taking some responsibility for the success of the interaction. If I read a book and, having made a moderate effort, can't make any sense of it, I probably place some blame on the author's side as well as acknowledging that I may not be the right audience. If I hear someone using a slur and am upset by it – if someone uses 'gay' as an insult, for example – I might go so far as to place all the blame on their rudeness.

In Quaker settings, I sometimes hear people who are upset by words for God treating them as if they are slurs. Sometimes there is a foundation for this. For example, a woman who would be offended to be called a bitch might also be offended when God is referred to as Father, Lord, or King. In the same way that she could place all the blame in the first case on the rude speaker, she might place all the blame in the second case on the person who chooses this language for the Divine. This reaction does capture the way in which this kind of language can be hurtful. Feminist writers have established clearly that, especially in contexts where only masculine language is used of the Divine, this is damaging to women. The hurt produced is social as well as emotional.

What this reaction, treating the specific words for God as if they were a slur, sometimes struggles to acknowledge is that this kind of language can also be useful. Some people, men and women alike, find the metaphor of God as Father protective and comforting – some because it relates to a positive relationship they had with their own father, some because it is the language used of God in their childhoods, and some because the image of the parent, mother or father, has connotations of love, care, and nurturing. Similarly, some people are able to read the metaphor of God as King in a positive way – for example, it can be politically subversive (God rules above any earthly power, whether monarch or Prime Minister).

If listening is an action as suggested by the story about Woolman and Papunehang, how should we respond when language Quakers use about God is upsetting? What would it look like to listen more deeply in this way?

Firstly, there's no point pretending not to be upset. Papunehang listens to where the words come from – he does not claim to have suddenly learned to understand English. Sharing an honest reaction, your genuine experience, can contribute to the process of truth-telling.

Secondly, the remarks need to be taken in context. Papunehang uses a translator at some times, but not for spoken ministry, distinguishing between different kinds of speech.

Taking a full picture of the context might involve thinking about the differences between ministry during worship and a discussion group, considering any positive connotations of the term involved as well as the negative aspects, and also asking whether this is a pattern used by this particular speaker or group, or a one-off, perhaps a quotation.

Thirdly, we are not observers but participants in a Quaker meeting. Papunehang, like anyone at a meeting for worship, is participating through his listening just as much as any of the ministers do by their speaking. Active listening, and where appropriate speaking out using our own preferred language, is a way to bring a balance to the community's wider patterns of language use. I'll be returning to this point in the chapter on new words.

Telling our stories

In the previous chapter, I identified the need to look at the whole context of a comment in order to listen to it carefully. Part of that context is the previous story of a word. I think that the story of a word operates at two levels. There's the big story, by which I mean the historical and cultural context of a word or phrase which can encompass thousands of years and many changes. Then there's the individual story, the personal background which involves how someone came to know and use a word and what they feel about it. In order to illustrate this, I'll use the word 'Spirit' as an example. In the big story about the word 'Spirit', we've got Christian uses – the term 'Holy Spirit', and behind it older translations, like 'Holy Ghost'. There are things about the Trinity, in which the Holy Spirit is one of three. There are connections with Jewish theology, because the New Testament Greek word we translate as 'Spirit' is itself a translation of a Hebrew word. There are the linguistic connections of those words with other meanings, like 'breath' and 'soul'.

I didn't know all that when I was young and learned to use the word 'Spirit', though. I grew up as a Quaker and I learned to use the word 'Spirit' in Quaker patterns – some of them descended from the Quaker part of the big story, like the ways early Friends used Christian language, and some relatively modern. I learned to use the word 'Spirit' on its own, as well as in phrases like 'Holy Spirit' or 'Spirit of Christ'. I learned to use phrases like 'the movement of the Spirit' and 'Spirit-led' – and, of course, to use the word in other phrases, like 'the spirit is willing but the flesh is weak'. When I use the word now all these meanings are present for me. For the word 'Spirit', these associations or connotations are relatively positive for me: it's a familiar, comfortable word, and I can carry that feeling even into settings where I am uncomfortable with other parts of the group's theology.

The same process can produce very different effects if the individual has different experiences. For example, people who have rejected a particular church or community might, as I described above, reject a word, or a whole set of words, which went with it. This often includes a rejection of some theological concept which is objectionable – many Quakers have strong negative reactions to any idea of 'salvation', especially a salvation which includes some and excludes others. I've seen people reduced to tears by a workshop exercise in which they are asked to reply to questions such as, 'Can people from other religions be saved?' In Quaker thought, salvation – usually understood not as a life after death but as the possibility of transformation, to bring one's life into line with the movement of the Spirit – is not limited to one group, and the concept of 'other' religions barely makes sense. The universalist idea that all religions point to the same truth is very deeply embedded. It is also very attractive to some who are repelled by the exclusive claims made by other religious communities. (Quakers are usually happy with the idea that religious groups we disagree with count as 'other'. From this we learn that we are capable of both irony and hypocrisy!)

If Quakers as a community are to move forward on the issue of religious language, we need to listen to and understand these stories, big and small. Sometimes an outline will be enough to give us the hints we need about how people might react – a Friend in my local meeting gives spoken ministry in language I find so patriarchal as to be almost entirely irrelevant to my way of thinking, but I know that her dual-belonging with a Roman Catholic church means that it is also very much alive for her. At other times, it is useful to dig down into the specifics of a particular word. Another Friend spent time over a cup of tea explaining why she finds hierarchical terms for God, like 'Lord', useful and powerful because they are politically subversive, rather than problematic. I wasn't convinced enough to start routinely using them in that way myself, but now I am able to hear this potential in them when she, or someone else, uses them.

To engage with stories in this way does take time. Ideally it is reciprocal, with both sides able to share something about their stories. It can help to relate the personal story to the historical and cultural background: growing up in a Quaker family in a largely Protestant society, I knew Mary as a character in the Christmas story but it would never have occurred to me to pray to her directly. Actually, it wasn't until I discovered Latin prayers to Mary being used in a neo-Pagan context, where Goddess worship was the focus, that I really understood this as a possibility with my heart rather than my head. The way in which Mary is left out of some Christian traditions and included in some post-Christian ones is part of the 'big story'; my discovery of *Ave Maria* as a Goddess chant is the point at which the big story touches my personal story.

I sometimes use a workshop exercise which I call 'Naming the Mystery', in which small groups can bring out these stories by sharing the words they use and don't use for God, and then asking each other about them. I begin by drawing two concentric circles on a big sheet of paper, so that there are three sections. The middle, the 'bullseye', I label ALWAYS: this is for the words we are confident about, and would use in any setting. The strip between the two circles becomes SOMETIMES: words which are contextual, which we might use, for example, among Quakers but not with others, or in prayer but not out loud. Finally, the area outside the circles is called NEVER. This might actually become two areas, because there are two kinds of words I never use to name God: words I don't know, and words I've rejected.

Groups begin by writing down their words, each person putting their own words onto sticky notes and into the correct sections of the diagram. When this begins to slow down – although some people always go on thinking of other words until the end of the exercise and beyond! – I ask them to look for patterns in what has been written. A common pattern is to have duplicates in some sections: Quaker groups often have a favourite word, like 'Light', over and over. Another common pattern is to have the same word in all three sections: someone in the group uses the word 'Christ' always, while another only uses it sometimes, and someone else rejects it entirely. It's also common to find that the 'never' category contains a whole set of words in which God seems to be angry, bossy, or judgemental. These patterns point to some of the stories I described above, and I encourage groups to be curious. They can ask questions like: Where did you learn that word? You put that word in SOMETIMES, so when do you use it and when do you avoid it? This word is in NEVER, but what is it about this word that you reject?

In this exercise, participants frequently learn new words from one another. Just about every word in the English language might be used as a name or metaphor for God, so there are thousands of possibilities before even beginning on other languages. This process can be both exciting and disorientating, as I explore in the next section.

New words for new light

Sometimes groups or individuals find that the words they have inherited are no longer doing the job: they have reached a point where current language no longer seems adequate and either new terms have to be coined or existing words have to be repurposed. This happens anyway, because people are endlessly creative. Sometimes, though, it feels like a continuity – a tradition evolving – and at other times it feels like a break, something new emerging. It's not always simple to say which is which, either: the development of 'txt speak' in which words are heavily abbreviated, often to only their key consonants, is an example. It happened under particular technological conditions (namely, a system in which reducing the number of letters in a message could drastically reduce both the financial and time costs involved in sending it), and was socially associated with a particular group (young people). Many who were not in that group spoke of it as if it were a break from all previous traditions, often expressing fears that it would lead to a wider breakdown in communication, because it seemed to be so different from standard patterns. From another perspective, though, it was a very obvious evolution of linguistic patterns which already existed in English. It can be put into a broader context and made to seem like a continuity by comparing it with the standard abbreviations which arose when people used telegrams regularly, for example, or with casual letter-writing habits such as signing off 'SWALK' (sealed with a loving kiss – the method is even the same as that used to produce 'LOL', laughed out loud).

In this section, then, I am not going to say that Quakers have ever fully broken from a previous tradition, since the traces of previous patterns are always to be found, but nor am I going to argue that every development was so natural as to be inevitable.

Instead, the sense of break or continuity is better located in the individual story, and I'm going to move towards looking at the big story. For some, the changes described here will have felt like a real break in the tradition, while for others the progression will seem to flow easily. There is also a theological dimension to this: on the one hand, continuity is part of being a religious tradition and honouring the revelations received by previous generations, while on the other hand, new developments are to be expected in a tradition which accepts continuing revelation through direct access to the Divine.

There have been a number of developments of this kind – I have already mentioned some, such as the move away from using masculine language for the Divine, and I will be returning to that later as well as raising others, such as the issue of whether language about God implies a transcendent God or one who is part of the human world. A particularly clear example is the move from personal language in which God is compared to a human being, to impersonal language in which God can be called 'Energy' or 'Universe' as well as 'Light' and other terms.

It's important to acknowledge here that some words with very common currency among Quakers are ambiguous about this. The word 'Spirit' – almost always just that, and very rarely 'Holy Spirit' – could be as personal as a soul or as impersonal as the wind. It's also been said before that the shift from 'Inward Light' (coming in from somewhere) to 'Inner Light' (starting off within the person) marks a shift in Quaker theological understanding about the location of the Divine, which could be tied in with many other changes. 'Light' on its own, though, I consider to be impersonal. It would be possible to personify light but it's equally possible to make the metaphor a very scientific one: as Joycelyn Burnell does in her Swarthmore lecture, in which she suggests that like light, which sometimes has to be described as a wave and sometimes as a particle, God might be correctly understood in more than one way.

There is also a sense in which this is part of a wider trend in some Christian thinking. The term 'ground of being', which now pops up sometimes in Quaker contexts, began with Paul Tillich, a very influential German Lutheran theologian working in the first half of the twentieth century. Ideas of this kind were most successfully popularised in English by John Robinson's 1963 book *Honest to God*, and Quakers were more receptive to them than many other churches at the time.

In general, this is typical of the appearance of new words in Quaker contexts. Sometimes Quakers create completely new uses of a word, but much more often they borrow a word from another tradition and make it their own. The process of making it a Quaker word can, just as when English absorbs a word from another language, include changes of grammar. Shades of meaning can be lost or gained, as when 'the Holy Spirit' becomes detached from the Trinity and absorbed into Quaker thought as 'the Spirit' which moves in meeting for worship. It is usually possible to trace the connections, though, and this means that Quakers stay connected in some ways to the 'big stories' even as we are also telling our own story.

Unity and Diversity: all the words in one big list

Another creative way in which Quakers have responded to the need to speak about God in new words is the use of the list of apparent synonyms. Before I go on to say more about lists, let me give you a few real examples of things Quakers have written so that you know what I'm talking about.

We have many names for the Divine—Spirit, God, Heavenly Father, Universe, Papa, Mother, Light—and we know that without it this work would not have been possible (The editors of *Spirit Rising: Young Quaker Voices*, 2010).

This [mystical experience] is the experience which has been given such names as 'God', 'The Light', 'The Tao', 'The Inward Christ', 'The Spirit', and 'that of God in everyone'. It is not the naming which is important but the experience (John Lampen, *Quaker Experience and Language*).

'God' is shorthand for that which is eternal: Being, Essence, Is-ness. Some would call this Light, or Love, or Christ (Peter Parr, *Answering that of God*, 2012). God or whatever we may choose to call it (Rex Ambler, *The End of Words*, 1994).

God or whatever we may choose to call it. (Rex Ambler, *The End of Words*, 1994)

In each of these lists – and these are just a few of many – lots of words are brought together to try and name God in a way which is acceptable to a wide range of theological views. All of them take it for granted that there is only one thing which lots of words can name, and they treat all the names as synonyms. Even when the words might be thought to name things with very different properties (some personal and some impersonal, some inward and some outward, some from traditions with entirely separate histories), the structure of the list brings them all together.

For Quakers, there are major advantages to this. The list helps the community to maintain, and even celebrate, both unity and diversity at the same time. By bringing everyone's words together (and even including those whose words you have forgotten by making it clear that those mentioned are only a sample and you can call 'it' whatever else you like) the list it creates brings people together. It treats all their words as equal and shows – or perhaps just makes it sound like – everyone coming to the same point behind the words, even if they disagree on 'surface' matters, like language.

At the same time, it makes everyone welcome and puts the diversity of the community on display. It makes a point of naming at least some of the differences which are present, and that can be a very powerful way of making people feel included. The list of words for God is a kind of speech act: like naming a ship or speaking wedding vows, it doesn't just describe a situation but makes something happen. When Quakers use lists of words for God we aren't just reflecting the community we are in, but actively creating one in which both diversity and unity are important values.

At the same time, the list isn't as absolutely inclusive as all that. For example, it assumes that the God it names – personal or impersonal, external or a human creation – is singular. Even as it includes nontheists who do not believe in some of the forms of God which it can also include, it assumes that the God they don't believe in is a monotheistic God. This doesn't come to light very often, because most in the Quaker community are happy enough with this assumption. The list does not, though, include polytheists. In some ways, a list of gods should suit the inclusion of polytheism, but these lists are always structured as lists of synonyms for one headword, rather than lists of many entities. (This is not to say that polytheists are not, or should not be, welcome in the Quaker community; there already are a few Quaker polytheists. It does mean that while soft polytheists

– who think many gods emanate from or represent elements of one ultimate reality – are likely to be comfortable enough, hard polytheists – who believe in many deities that are completely separate and distinct – are likely to be aware at some level that their understanding is in conflict with the general Quaker picture of the world.)

All being equal in the list isn't as brilliant as it might first appear, either. There's still the possibility that all the understandings included by using the list are equally wrong. The list affirms unity and diversity, and less explicitly monotheism. It doesn't make truth claims about any of the ideas it includes. If you think that your belief about God goes beyond a private opinion to a claim which everyone should share, being included in the list is like being invited to a really boring party. It might be better than not being invited, but you're going to be wishing for a lot more.

The list of words for God, then, is a fairly minimal level of theological talk. The widespread use of it, though, does show that Quakers are trying to find ways to build shared understandings in the middle of all these diverse beliefs. It also means that it's reasonable to expect Quakers to be able to offer other items which they could put on a list. This is assumed in a number of exercises which have been suggested for Quaker discussion groups over the years, and it's at the heart of my 'Naming the Mystery' exercise. People can only sort their words for God into ALWAYS, SOMETIMES, and NEVER if they are able to think of plenty of words which could be about God in the first place.

In order to explore the items which appear in the lists in more detail, I want to move on now to look at discussions around some particular groups of words: Christian words, especially those about Jesus, and Buddhist words.

Putting Jesus in his place(s)

A workshop group who had tried the 'Naming the Mystery' exercise once pointed out to me an interesting pattern on their sheet. The words 'Jesus' and 'Christ' both appeared in both the ALWAYS and the NEVER categories. One woman explained that she associated the name 'Jesus' with the Jesus of history, whom she could accept as a wise teacher, and whose name she was consequently comfortable using, while she associated the word 'Christ' with the supernatural claims which, she felt, had been added onto the teaching by later believers and which in some cases, such as the Virgin Birth, had damaging implications. She'd put 'Jesus' into the 'always' category and 'Christ' into the 'never' category.

Another woman, however, explained that her pictures of 'Jesus' and 'Christ' were very different. To her, 'Christ' was the mystical, universal aspect of the figure of the Son of God – something inward, spiritual, and accessible to all – while 'Jesus' was the physical incarnation who had little relevance to today and whose followers made specific claims about him as an individual which excluded those from other cultures and those who couldn't accept certain beliefs. She'd put 'Christ' into the 'always' category and 'Jesus' into the 'never' category.

Someone else had, understandably, put the phrase 'Jesus Christ' into the 'sometimes' category!

One of the ways in which people sometimes feel that the liberal Quaker tradition today has broken away from its roots is with the shift away from using traditionally Christian language. It's easy to point to multiple causes for this – other Christian churches are still struggling with the patriarchal implications of much traditional Christian language; Quakers today, like many others, are less familiar with the Bible and other Christian sources, and so look to other places for their inspiration; and

Christianity traditionally has a very personal God, revealed through a historic Jesus, and miracles, and other elements with which some Quakers today are not at all comfortable. In this section, however, I am more interested in the ways Quakers do accept some parts of Christianity, without wanting to take it all.

A very shallow example of this is the Quaker return to celebrating Christmas (and sometimes some other Christian festivals). At one time, Quakers rejected times and seasons, saying that every day is equally special. Early Quakers were sometimes arrested for trading on Sundays – all days are equal – and they did not mark Christmas, Easter, or other church festivals. Today, however, most Quakers do participate. It is a tradition much more honoured in the breach than the observance, almost as if one has to do some Christmassy things (buying a few presents, singing the theological agreeable parts of a few carols, and perhaps making some seasonal charity donations) in order to be reminded of what it is one isn't doing. From one perspective, this could be seen as a process of capitulation to social norms – 'everyone else' (mainly the more-or-less Christian people who form the bulk of society, and not including, for example, most of the Jewish community) is doing it, so Quakers join in. This is especially plausible when many Quakers have non-Quaker families who place clear expectations on people to participate in rituals such as gift-giving.

From another perspective, however, this is a Quaker acceptance that some elements of Christianity, even those previously rejected, do have a place in the tradition. Quakers may be celebrating Christmas because everyone else is, but they are also doing it 'for the children' – not just as a result of social pressure, but because they see a teaching opportunity. Quaker celebrations of Christmas are only partly on the standard model: they sing carols, but choose which verses based on theological principles as well as nostalgia; the children of the meeting may produce a nativity play, but it's as likely to be a modernised version in which the refugee family fleeing to Egypt hammer home an ethical message about welcoming the stranger as a dramatization of the words from a Gospel.

Moving away from the issue of Christmas, what other places does Jesus Christ have in Quakerism today? As suggested by the workshop participants, there are two main understandings of Jesus which are broadly acceptable to Quakers. (There are many, many more which are accepted by some Quakers – and a reminder here that I am talking mainly about British Quakers and therefore the liberal tradition within Quakerism.) These are Jesus as teacher, and Christ as spirit.

To see Jesus as a teacher does not require any supernatural beliefs. It can be compatible with them – with the view of Christ as spirit described below, for example – but it can also rest solely on the idea that there was a historical Jesus who had some good ideas. Jesus the teacher is recorded in the Gospels, and most people who take this position would say that these contain some elements of truth. Not the miracles (or at least, the miracles are symbolic rather than physical happenings), but the content of the parables, the Sermon on the Mount, and so on. As might be expected, this is a view of Jesus which is popular with those who also reject other supernatural elements – who, for example, do not accept a Divine who exists outside the human frame of reference. What is less expected, perhaps, is that the popularity of this view sometimes makes it seem that Jesus (the human teacher Jesus) is actually more important to Quakers who do not accept supernatural elements than to some of those who are happy with an externally real but not very specific Divine.

The view of Christ as spirit is a long standing Quaker one, and those Quakers who adopt it today can easily find early Quaker writings which support the idea that what is significant about Jesus Christ is not so much his historical life – although some will also accept the importance of that – but his living presence in the world today. I have phrased it as 'Christ as spirit' not with the intention of giving those familiar with traditional Trinitarian teachings the jitters, although I know it might have that effect, but to connect this idea with the emphasis on the Spirit which is widely found in Quakerism today. Quakers do not usually distinguish the spiritual Christ, living and present with us, from the Spirit, or the Inner Light, or other expressions which focus on the personal experience of connection. If they do pick out something specific about Christ in this context, it is often that the Inward Christ is an inward teacher – a move which makes this view especially compatible with the view of Jesus as teacher described above. As with many other Quaker theological claims, the claims about metaphysics (the nature of the world beyond the directly observable) are, or can be, relatively weak. Christ might be an incarnation of an external Deity, transcendent beyond time and space and 'real' in a hard, out-there, physical sense. Equally well, this Christ might be an archetypal aspect of the human being, non-material like love between people but just as much part of the human world.

Neither of these understandings of Jesus Christ lead to any claim that he forms an exclusive path of access to God (or heaven, or salvation – not, as I've noted before, concepts on which Quakers spend much time). Even Quakers who do think that Jesus was a particularly good teacher, maybe even the best, can accept the usefulness of teachings from other sources, and even those who think that understanding Christ as spirit will enhance a person's spiritual life can also say that other descriptions using other words can also be effective. In this way, there is both space for Christian teachings in Quakerism and an underlying acceptance of universalism.

Connecting to the big story: Quakers and Buddhism

So far, when I have been talking about the 'big story', the cultural and historical background from which our words for God derive, I have drawn my examples from Christianity and from the European traditions. Quakers have always been open to other traditions, though – George Fox and Margret Fell, founding members of the Quaker movement, took an active if sometimes patronising interest in Judaism and Islam. In an increasingly globalised world, and often living in multicultural societies, Quakers today have more access than ever before to wisdom from other religious traditions. This can bring with it great riches, which Quakers have been quick to see and to use, a move which one might see as repeating colonial patterns especially where the sources are simultaneously treated as 'foreign' and 'exotic'. It can also bring with it theological questions, such as the issue of whether concepts from another belief system are really compatible with those already present in Quakerism, and practical educational issues about what people should do when the words of their preferred tradition are strange to those with whom they are worshipping.

The workshop exercises already described in this book might provide answers to some of the second point. In particular, it can help us to understand the personal parts of the story: I might not need to know much of the history or cultural context of the figure of Green Tara in order to understand that a friend of mine, who found a Green Tara meditation very comforting in a time of spiritual crisis, values the name and image of Green Tara. My friend can tell me about his experience of feeling protected from delusions by Green Tara, but he might or might not be able to fill me in about the 'big story' of Green Tara's followers and interpretations.

Does that matter? If all that is at stake is the friendship, probably not. However, a community – even the Religious Society of Friends – is made up of more than just individual friendships. The group needs to be able to explain our shared practices to ourselves and to newcomers. If my friend explains 'what happens in meeting for worship' in terms which draw on his experience of Green Tara, I probably do need to understand some of the wider context within which the figure of Green Tara exists in order to be able to see whether or not his explanation is consistent with my own, or with those offered by other people. (Shouldn't I be listening to what is behind the words? I can, but I will still need to understand the words as well – this is a discussion, communication between people, not a message from God or Green Tara.)

At the moment, the model for engagement with other traditions seems to be that of multiple religious belonging. As my friend practises both Quakerism and Tibetan Buddhism, so other people work with more than one tradition and act as conduits through which ideas flow between the different contexts. The community relies for information on a low level of general knowledge and being given specific points by the individuals who are using words or concepts from another tradition. Among the advantages to this are that it is practical, inclusive, accepting, flexible, and places no obligation on other community members. However, it also places a burden of education (both to learn and to teach) on individuals, risks losing the shared story of the community, and can distort much of what is borrowed to make it 'fit' the new context.

It would be tempting at this point to recommend that Quakers should create group study practices in which the community could come together to learn about the traditions from which some of their members are drawing. I am well aware, though, that it would be impractical: Quakers have been suggesting for many years that the community would benefit from more engagement with biblical studies and Christianity. There are small pockets where this happens – local meetings who have a Bible reading group, for example – but it has not been generally taken up, and to add something else which ought to be studied, but won't be, seems like a waste of effort. Instead, I want to turn to an area where a group did succeed in making a change in the ways Quakers speak about God: the Quaker Women's Group, whose feminist views did affect Quaker use of gendered language for the Divine.

Pronouns and beyond

The Fatherhood of God, as revealed by Jesus Christ, should lead us toward a brotherhood which knows no restriction of race, sex or social class.

In 1918, Quakers meeting in London were able to approve these words as the first of eight 'Foundations of a True Social Order'. (The document giving all eight is printed in full in *Quaker faith & practice*, as section 23.16, and explored with further historical background on the 'Reimagining a True Social Order' website.) They were responding to war, revolution, and calls for social change. Clearly they were in some ways aware of the discrimination women faced merely because of their gender, but at the same time they reaffirmed the masculinity of God in his 'Fatherhood' and assumed that a 'brotherhood' would include all. In the 1980s and early 1990s, the committee who decided to include it in *Quaker faith & practice* also decided to include an introductory passage – unusual, even in the chapters which collect anthology material from a wide range of sources – which ends with the sentence: 'Though they proclaimed the ending of "restrictions" of sex, they spoke of God as Father and human beings as men and brothers, as was conventional in their time.'

The implication of this is that by the time that was approved in 1994 – by the same meeting of British Quakers who had approved it in the 1918 wording – the use of such phrases was no longer conventional. If anything, it might be truer to say that it was still conventional in some parts of society, but no longer acceptable to Quakers or others who valued equality between people. In line with that, it seems that gendered language for human beings is quicker to drop out than gendered language for God – something perhaps echoed in other churches, where the ordination of women has not led to a widespread abandonment of masculine terms (especially, but not only, 'Father' and 'Son').

Quakers today generally recognise a need to avoid masculine language for the Divine in formal contexts. Although the term 'God' has a feminine counterpart in English, 'Goddess', this seems to have gone the way of some other feminine equivalents – male and female writers are all 'authors' now, even though 'authoress' can be found in dictionaries. Other favourite Quaker terms, such as 'Light', 'Love', and 'Spirit', are clearly gender-neutral. In a lecture given to those present at Yearly Meeting in 1986, the Quaker Women's Group shared some of the hurt which can result when God is seen as only masculine and therefore closer to men than women. This point was clearly heard. Although it takes a while for this to filter down to everyone in the Quaker community, the rejection of exclusively masculine language for God is now so widespread among Quakers that it is only in reading historical texts that one realises it was once present.

A few Quakers have suggested using feminine language instead. 'G-d/ess' appears in one passage in the 1994 *Quaker faith & practice* – but it was controversial, required a follow-up passage explaining the usage, and has not been taken up widely. Some places which list words for God attempt balance by including 'mother' alongside 'father', but this seems to be an artefact of list-making as I do not hear this used in general. Indeed, in workshops, Quaker participants sometimes tell me that they specifically reject feminine words for the Divine for the same reasons as masculine ones. In particular, they identify as a problem the way in which calling God 'father' encourages people to imagine God as like their own human father, and point out that human mothers can also be difficult to live with, neglectful, or abusive.

The personal: the stories of words in our lives

As well as belonging to big cultural and historical stories, the words we use are part of our individual and everyday stories. They connect us with our communities – sometimes via the 'big stories' and sometimes through intermediate stories in a family or local group. This might take the form of an in-joke, where everyone knows what the phrase refers to: in some Quakers' groups, I can use 'or whatever you call it' to mean 'God', because everyone knows that the Divine is the thing you'd have too many names for to be able to list them all. In other settings, that wouldn't make any sense.

It can be difficult to notice our own uses sometimes. When I began doing the 'Naming the Mystery' exercise and asking people to put their words for God into categories called ALWAYS, SOMETIMES, or NEVER, I would have said confidently, along with many other Quakers, that I never use the word 'Lord' for God. At one level, that's true: I don't like the word or the implications it has, it seems old-fashioned and not really related to my experience of Divine presence, and so I don't want to use it. And yet, working with these issues over a period of years has made me aware that under some circumstances, I do use it.

I would never, I think, use it in a real prayer. I do use it, though, in joke prayers, in constructing a form which explains to people 'this is a prayer' even when I am not serious: for example, when people ask me what it's like to facilitate workshops alone, I often say that I begin the session with a silent prayer: 'Oh Lord, send me an even number of participants.' When you have to split people into pairs and small groups, prime numbers can seem like the work of the devil!

And there I go again – I don't believe in a devil in any straightforward way, and yet I'm happy to use the word, and the figure, to make a joke.

Besides these jesting uses of 'Lord', I also use it seriously at times, usually when someone else has chosen the words for me. I volunteer regularly with a Brownie group. Although the Girl Guiding movement in the UK has got rid of the word 'God' from the Promise (members promise instead to 'be true to myself and develop my beliefs'), every group I know still sings a closing prayer to the tune of the Westminster chimes: 'Oh Lord our God, thy children call; grant us thy peace and bless us all.' I sang it when I was seven and became a Brownie, and I sing it with children now. It bothers me a bit. It doesn't bother me enough to stop me participating in this practice, which serves an important social function – giving a shared, recognised group end to a meeting – and links the group to the wider religious story which is an important part of our cultural heritage.

I might also be considered to use the word 'Lord' extensively in writing a section like this one. This is a bit different, though – a difference philosophers describe as the use/mention distinction. Under this distinction, it's possible to mention a word (like 'Lord', or perhaps a slur, like 'bitch') without using it. It isn't until you're applying it to something or someone that you are really using it. In writing, I can make this distinction with so-called 'scare quotes': putting the word 'Lord' into quotation marks distinguishes it from addressing the Lord directly. Or I can put it in the NEVER category on my diagram: mentioning it as a possible word in a discussion does not count as using the word in the full sense.

Some of these uses of the word 'Lord' point to the places where I would have learned it. I don't have a specific memory of encountering this word for the first time – I don't think it would have been used much in the Quaker meeting in which I grew up, but it featured in some songs we sang in primary school assembly, and in songs and prayers I learned at Brownies. I do remember, for example, that there was a poster in the church hall with the words of the Lord's Prayer, which I disliked but somehow found intriguing enough that I memorised it. For me, these were mostly puzzling encounters, neutral or positive, and presented as possibilities rather than rules. I felt able to reject what I didn't like – including the Lord's Prayer – and enjoy what I did find nourishing – including any number of simple prayers and songs.

This personal history has two important effects: it positions me in a particular moment in the wider story of Christianity, and it shapes the way I feel (and perhaps even the way I think) about specific words, the practices which involve them, and the tradition from which they come. I have a very positive feeling about some of the simple prayers and songs I learned in childhood, and intellectual worries about the word 'Lord' are not enough to take away the pleasure I get from a song like 'Johnny Appleseed': 'The Lord is good to me, and so I thank the Lord, for giving me the things I need: the sun, the rain and the apple seed.'

It would be easy to regard this as unimportant: because it's childish, because it's about emotions and not at all 'spiritual', because the worries about the word are intellectual and not at all 'spiritual', because it's a positive feeling and those are allowed, because it's about my personal past and I should let go or move past it … It would be easy to regard this as unimportant, but all of these reasons for dismissing these facts ignore the crucial point: my history with, and resulting feelings about, a word or phrase do get carried through into my responses when someone else uses it, whether I like that or not. This can be more or less conscious. If anything, the more I am conscious of the process, the more I find I can set aside that history and respond to the speaker from a place of trying to understand their perspective. Setting something aside, though, is a temporary move – it isn't the same as putting it in the bin – so I still have those feelings.

That's one thing when the feelings are mainly positive. I am sometimes bothered by the contrast between positive feelings about and intellectual dislike of a word I find problematic, but what I am advocating – accepting and owning this process – is much more difficult if the emotions involved are strongly negative. When I hear stories from people who have experienced abusive churches, who associate some words for God with pain and fear and punishment and other horrible experiences, or have had very difficult experiences which involved the use (or misuse) of religious language, I'm not surprised that we struggle with this as a community. Not only are there people whose personal histories create very negative feelings around specific words for God, there are also people who struggle with the very concept – and those for whom it is the denial of God, or being told not to express themselves using specific words, which brings these negative connotations. When a community includes people in both these positions, there's likely to be conflict unless the different experiences can be brought out into the open enough for everyone to understand what is happening and why.

Understanding these possibilities and finding ways to support people who have good reason to find it very difficult to hear particular words or views is a challenge. I was going to say that it's a challenge for all those involved in providing pastoral care within the Quaker community, but in a community where everyone should be involved – whether or not they are presently serving in an appointed role to make sure pastoral care is provided – it really is a challenge for the whole community. I think that we have to begin by telling these stories, not as a one-off but as part of an ongoing process in which we are always working to get to know one another better.

Not God

It's all very well to have lots of words for God if you think that there is something worth naming as God. It's all very well to explore how people feel about words for God, but it doesn't address a key point in the matter of telling the truth about God. What if there is no God?

This is a place where I need to begin with a series of denials. There are several kinds of God which Quakers usually don't believe in anyway, and then there are some kinds of God which they may or may not believe in, and then the question of what Quakers who don't believe in any kind of God can believe in.

It's an old saw that everyone is already an atheist about the gods of ancient Greece and Rome. It isn't entirely true, since there are both reconstructionist polytheists who seek to believe much as the ancients did, and modern polytheists who incorporate these deities into another belief structure – although I note that the latter group includes some who would, by the Quaker uses of the terms, be nontheists, since they think that the gods they believe in are metaphors or archetypes. It does, however, get at a truth, which is that for every god someone does believe in, there are usually several they don't.

Some universalist positions sound like they believe in all the gods going, but on investigation it usually becomes clear that what is actually happening is that all the other gods are believed to be expressions of whatever the believer thinks is really there. Seeing all religions as different ways of expressing the same truth is very appealing, especially to Quakers who value open-mindedness and equality. However, it can be easy for this to slip into either intellectual dishonesty, where the claim to sameness elides or disguises real differences of opinion, and/or a kind of religious colonialism, where the assumption that the universalist knows better than those who have particular religious beliefs allows people to act superior to those they are trying to treat as equal.

Quakers, in general, do not believe in a God who is exclusive. We do not believe in a God who speaks to us and not to them: only that *they*, whoever they are, are not listening properly. We believe in a God which can guide – but this might be blindly, as following the flow of a river guides you towards the sea, just as much as it might be knowingly, as being given a set of directions guides you to your destination. It might be a co-creation, as a map might guide you without knowing your destination in advance. Quakers do not believe in a God which is closed off: one person might report the experience of direct connection with the Divine while another does not, but the gate into access to God is opened from the human side.

For some Quakers, that has to be the case because God is universal. For others, that has to be the case because God is human.

Here, the question about God gets tangled up with several other issues, of which the top two are materiality and transcendence. The question about materiality is: what kinds of non-physical things exist? Particularly important is the issue of whether the human mind or soul has a non-physical existence, somehow separate from even if always happening at the same time as the existence of the human body. Some non-physical things can easily be named and accepted even within a view which says that only the material world exists: fictional characters can be named and discussed, and exist as fictional characters, through purely physical mechanisms. The question about transcendence is: how far 'beyond' or 'outside' you does something have to be in order to be really transcending? In this case, people slide between talking about an external reality (external to what? me? the universe?) and talking about something which is either non-physical or perhaps supernatural. The non-physical need not be supernatural – Sherlock Holmes gains his wide recognition as a fictional character through entirely mundane means – and the supernatural need not be transcendent – ghosts could, if they exist at all, exist purely within the material world.

Different Quakers make many and varied claims about their beliefs in this area. Sometimes these arise from logic, as when someone denies the existence of the supernatural because there is no evidence for it. Sometimes these arise from feeling, as when someone accepts that they saw a ghost of their mother because it is comforting to do so. Sometimes these arise from childhood training, or faith, or hope, or a combination of the above. Rather than try to generalise about Quaker belief based on the explicit claims we make, I think it's better to look at the ways Quakers behave – both in community actions and in what is said implicitly – for clues about what kind of God we really think we are dealing with.

Quakers act as if we believe that something more than ego and really present in the world can guide a decision making process. We continue to gather in meeting for worship for business to discern what to do as a group. That process involves acting as if the Guide can be accessed through a process of getting together and listening carefully. It does not involve a commitment to where exactly this Guide is located, and even those Quakers most staunchly committed to there being no 'real' God continue to use this process – as I learned when I sat in on the AGM of the Nontheist Friends Network.

Quakers also typically speak as if all words for what happens in meeting for worship are provisional and metaphorical. Even those most committed to using words like God, Christ, Light, or Father would agree that such language is not a complete and final expression of the Divine nature. Many of them would suggest that God is ineffable, unable to be understood let alone explained by human minds – which is still possible even if God is in some way part of the human mind, since we also can't explain in any detail how the firing of brain cells adds up to consciousness and thought. Furthermore, Quakers typically hold the common sense position that words do not express the whole truth – that there is some meaning beyond a word which can be listened to but not said. The word 'red' might describe a red object, but it doesn't – can't – express everything about what it is like to look at something red.

In order for it to make sense to bring words for God together into a list, as Quaker writers repeatedly do, it has to be the case that none of them are the final word. (Some versions of the list even end with ... or tail off into 'or whatever you call it' in order to avoid having a literal final word.) The process of denial after denial always means that for anything someone affirms, there will be someone else ready to raise a question about it. In these ways, Quaker truth telling about God builds into the process an element of doubt. This means that there is always space for those who, in the short or the long term, do not believe in 'God'.

In everyone

A well-used – perhaps over-used! – Quaker phrase concerns 'that of God in everyone'. This entered the Quaker phrasebook because George Fox used it in a letter once, but it has been picked up and quoted and re-quoted until it sometimes seems that it is the closest thing Quakers have to a written creed. It ties together two core ideas: the image of the Inner Light, through which God can speak, and the idea that everyone is equal and valuable, sometimes rephrased as 'the good in everyone'.

From my description so far, I think it's fairly clear that this idea is compatible with a wide range of other beliefs. For example, believers and nontheists alike can use the phrase, because to say that there is something of God in people does not lay down whether there is also something of God outside people. Some Quakers who don't accept anything transcending the universe but are happy to have 'that of God' go beyond individuals might also talk about a kind of collective unconscious, in which our individual 'bits of God' can communicate. Another view could say that it is in the practice of meeting for worship that we bring our individual 'that of God' forward into consciousness and hence into communion with others present.

Whichever of the many claims about God's nature you accept or don't, it is also clear that the phrase 'that of God in everyone' is deeply humanistic. Like other forms of religious humanism – which may or may not be atheistic – it brings God and people so close together that for many purposes, it may not be necessary, if it is even possible, to distinguish them. This also conforms to a view of God's action in the world which is widely held by Quakers as well others: God has no hands but ours. Again, this is compatible with a more or less metaphysical – beyond the material – picture of God. It also retains the focus on humanity as the significant, and perhaps the only, location of God.

For believers from other churches or faith traditions this kind of talk can sound blasphemous. It just is obvious to many that God must be transcendent, eternal, all-loving, omnipotent, and so forth. The idea that some Quakers might believe in a God which is limited to action through human hands, which leads a group without having a plan or a personality, who might not be able to get through if people stopped listening, raises the question: is this really God anymore? In order to be worth worshipping, does God not have to do a bit more than this?

Some Quakers give up using the term 'God' for just these reasons. They may or may not be happy to use it in Quaker-only spaces, or where it's clear that a Quaker interpretation is at work, but they think that using it in conversation with others just confuses the issue. The argument here is that the Quaker picture of what God is like is not only vague, but also so far removed from the way other groups usually use the word 'God' that it's bordering on misleading if you make it sound like Quakers believe the same thing as other religious groups.

The first point is that not all Quakers stop at the human-focussed God I have been describing here. I am trying to sketch the starting points, the things Quakers have in common, but there are many who would say much more. Lots of Quakers believe in a God who is all-loving, for example; many believe in miracles, telepathy, and mystical experiences which prove the existence of God. The Trinity presents a few problems if you try and fit it into the way Quakers ordinarily speak about God – because they put everything into a single list, the neatness of the Creator/Incarnation/Spirit pattern is lost – but otherwise conventional Christian doctrines are still compatible with this theology. They can even lead to the same place once the theology is worked through into ethics; Quakers are not unique in embracing pacifism and the full equality of same-sex relationships, for example.

More importantly, I don't see why we should lose the word

'God' to an over-specific use. Both some religious fundamentalists and some atheists would like God to be reduced to a very narrow picture – either one which supports their claim to authority, or one which can be completely disproved, thereby supporting other claims. Words, though, belong to everyone who uses the language. We can cope with differences of meaning in different contexts (the icon on my computer screen is not the same as the one on the church wall) and with developments over time. To use the word 'God' at least puts me in the right area, and once my topic has been classed with spirituality and religion and faith, I can then go on to clarify how I use that word.

Nor is it necessary to accept that the God I have sketched as a Quaker God is not 'strong' or 'big' enough to be called God. On the very same grounds that it is possible to object to the 'humanised' God of modern Quakerism, who seems to have come apart from traditional Christian thought and to be small and weak and hardly worth worshipping, it is possible to argue the opposite. The idea that God becomes human could be seen as the very core of the Christian story. To rule out the possibility that God is fully present in human action, or chooses to refrain from acting in other ways, is again to limit the picture of what God could be like.

Some years ago, the charity Christian Aid produced a poster campaign with the strapline, 'We believe in life before death.' I think Quakers at the moment are saying something similar about God. Any individual Quaker may not be sure whether God exists outside time, or outside the universe, or outside language, or outside people, but we affirm that something loving, guiding, and worth listening to is active now, here, in our community. And we call that something God, or the Divine, or the Light, or the Spirit, or the True Self, or the 'flowing vastness of presence', or the Ground of Being, or …

Saying Thou to we know not what

Where does all this leave the Quaker community?

Firstly, it leaves us agreeing to disagree. This isn't just about relationships within the community, but about establishing a rule of behaviour in which disagreeing is fine, but rejecting people because they disagree about theology is not okay. (When is it okay to reject people from the community? When they show no repentance and continue to break the behavioural creed, especially with something like violence which also conflicts with long-established Quaker values, or when they have views which make it clear that they wouldn't follow important behavioural norms like caring for one another.) Naming and living with the ongoing struggle to tell the truth about God – for individuals and for the group – is likely to become central to Quaker experience.

It leaves us trying to live in relationship with something we don't understand. This was actually the case anyway, whether you believe in God (who is ineffable) or don't (and need to try and understand what God-believers are on about). Martin Buber famously talked about the difference between a loving 'I/Thou' relationship and a formal 'I/You' relationship. It's not always a distinction which fits comfortably into Quaker thought, especially given our history of rejecting the you/thou distinction when it was applied to mark differences of social status among people, but it captures something about the need to live closely with whatever it is 'God' is. Being a practising Quaker is going to bring us back to that, over and over, regardless of our beliefs. In traditional language, this is the continuing attempt to pray: to say to Thou, who already knows, what is in our hearts.

It leaves us needing to learn to get these questions out in the open in our relationships with one another. Like prayer, a discussion with a friend is a chance to understand yourself better as well as become closer to your friend. In trying to summarise how this relationship will develop, I have sometimes said that we have to try, we have to cry, and we have to clarify. To open the process, we need to try and put into words our spiritual experiences and theological understandings. We don't have to succeed – we probably won't – but the relationship doesn't move to this level unless we try. The plural, 'we', is important here, too: it isn't enough that I've tried (even though you've bought my book). You have to try, and other members of the community have to try, or we will never build up a rounded picture.

Once someone has tried to express the truth about God as they have it, there's a good chance someone is going to be upset. It would be nice to think that this could be avoided, but in almost every case this personal, vulnerable, difficult, emotional, philosophical, wretched, vitally important topic is going to be upsetting. Just trying to put things into words may be enough to have this effect for some people, especially if they feel that their experience or perspective will not be valued. For others, hearing someone else's views may make them feel like they don't really belong in the community, or that they aren't 'good enough' or 'spiritual enough', or that what they hold dear is being talked down or misrepresented. If I thought there was a way to always avoid this, I would be recommending it. Instead, I have come to the conclusion that the best way to learn from this is to make it visible. It's easy for a community who want to feel happy and nice to skip over this stage and miss all the opportunities it provides. If you're upset, say so. If it makes you want to weep, weep. These are your own feelings, part of your picture of the truth, and you are allowed to feel them.

So your group has tried telling the truth about God, and been honest about how you feel: what next? Back to the beginning, or perhaps moving along the spiral. Descriptions of what God might be like, ways of naming the mystery, connections to personal and cultural-historical stories, can all be answers to questions but also raise further questions. The final step, then, is clarification. As in the first step, you have to try and express yourself. This time, though, some of the building blocks are in place and you can be more nuanced, deeper, more personal, more poetic. Over time, by cycling through these stages a community can come to understand one another's perspectives very clearly – which is not to suggest that they will ever agree!

In the process of talking to each other and getting to know our many individual stories, we will also be reshaping our relationship to the big, cultural-historical stories I have talked about. These relationships may be new contacts – our Quaker story getting to know another big story through the interactions provided by individuals who have been touched by both. These relationships may be difficult – old familiar ideas may no longer fit, or new ones might have unexpected effects. And some of these relationships will always be complex. For example, we are unlikely to either make a clean break from the huge story known as Christianity, because so much of our language and understanding and social context is drawn from it, or to fold completely back in to become just another Christian church, because there is so much which is distinctive (and, some Christians might say, heretical) about the Quaker movement. Seeing how our individual stories reflect this pattern of connection, rejection, and affection will help us to represent our relationships to other traditions honestly.

Representing our community honestly is also important because the ongoing process of trying to tell the truth about God is also one which affects how we present ourselves and how we are seen in the wider world. This includes the way we talk about our community when we describe it to enquirers and visitors at meeting, how we explain our reasons for taking collective public stands on everything from marriage and family life to economics and the use of finite resources, and how we interact with other faith communities. The kinds of listening processes – try, cry, clarify – which I suggested might be used within the Quaker community will also be relevant in some of these situations, although building a space in which everyone is safe enough to fully participate will be even more of a challenge.

Finally, though, all of this also leaves us ready to get on with it. I identified earlier that one of the characteristics of the Quaker God is that She, He, It, or They is a Guide. Theologising is an important process but it is one which happens alongside other things. We can theologise and at the same time act – indeed, some of the best ordinary theology I've ever heard has been created at times when a group of people came together around a common cause. We can tell the truth about God through campaigning, helping others, and compassion as well as through words. We can listen to and follow God in faith, seeing that good is happening, while questions about the exact nature of that God are still open. We can theologise amongst ourselves and at the same time theologise with others. Sometimes it's good to give our process of exploring stories dedicated time and attention, but it's also something you can do over the washing up.

How are you telling the truth about God?

After reading this book

If you would like to explore these questions further, this section suggests some resources you might find useful. In the comment on each one I explain why it might be of interest and who the intended audience is.

God, Words and Us: Quakers in conversation about religious difference, ed. Helen Rowlands, Quaker Books, 2017

A central British Quaker publication which resulted from a group of around twenty Quakers meeting to discuss their understandings of God. The short extracts often reflect the kind of story-telling process recommended in this book, and some of the key ideas I explore can also be found here – not least because I was a member of the group which produced it.

Naming the Mystery, a 'Being Friends Together' resource by Rhiannon Grant, available at http://together.woodbrooke.org.uk/session.php?s=T248

I created these videos, and the associated guidance on running workshop sessions, in 2015. They give detailed instructions for the exercises described in this book and other suggestions for holding discussions on this topic.

Quaker Renewal, Craig Barnett, The Friend Publications, 2017

This collection of short essays considers the state of Quakerism in Britain today, in particular suggesting that Quakers need to recover a shared story in order to form a stronger community. Craig Barnett also writes a blog, Transition Quaker, which includes other reflections on these themes, and can be found at http://transitionquaker.blogspot.co.uk/

'Openings', a blog by Sam Barnett-Cormack, https://quakeropenings.blogspot.co.uk/

Sam Barnett-Cormack identifies as a Quaker nontheist and sets out to explore aspects of Quakerism. His blog posts are often informative and aim to understand the perspectives of others.

Testimony: Quakerism and theological ethics, Rachel Muers, SCM
Press, 2015

Rachel Muers is both an academic theologian and a Quaker,
a position which enables her to bring Quaker tradition into
dialogue with other Christian insights. The understanding of
testimony she explores here is directly related to the idea of
truth-telling as used in this book.

An Introduction to Quakerism, Pink Dandelion, Cambridge
University Press, 2007

This is an overview book which covers Quaker history and
sociology. Pink Dandelion brings together a huge amount of
material in a rigorous way, and provides lots of references to
sources for those who want to go further. For those who would
like to read about Quaker history but find this book, aimed at
undergraduates, daunting, alternatives include John Punshon's
book *A Portrait in Grey: a short history of the Quakers* (Quaker
Home Service, 1984) or the regularly repeated free three-week
online course *Radical Spirituality*, hosted by Futurelearn and
created by Lancaster University with the Centre for Research in
Quaker Studies: https://www.futurelearn.com/courses/quakers

Godless for God's Sake, ed. David Boulton, Dales Historical
Monographs, 2006 and *The Faith of a Quaker Humanist*, David
Boulton, Dales Historical Monographs, 1997

David Boulton has written extensively on his understanding
of Quakerism, and these are not the most recent entries. However,
they stand as classics, and in particular *Godless for God's Sake*
plays an especially useful role in collecting a range of Quaker
nontheist views.

*The Beyond Within: A commentary on Through a Glass Darkly,
David Boulton's response to my A Man That Looks on Glass*, Derek
Guiton, FeedARead Publishing, 2017

As the subtitle of this volume suggests, it is not Derek Guiton's
first book on this subject. However, I would recommend it as
the best read: the process of debate seems to have sharpened

Guiton's points and streamlined his arguments.

Janet Scott, *What Canst Thou Say?* (Swarthmore Lecture), Quaker Home Service, 1980

The Swarthmore lectures – including this and the following three items – are an annual opportunity for a Quaker to expand their thinking in some detail. Janet Scott's explores several aspects of Quaker theology in a clear and helpful way.

Quaker Women's Group, *Bringing the Invisible into the Light: Some Quaker Feminists speak of their experience* (Swarthmore Lecture), Quaker Home Service, 1986

Given by a group rather than an individual, this lecture brought to the attention of the Yearly Meeting a lot which had been hidden, especially to men. It did not end sexism among Quakers but did have a visible impact on the ways we speak about God.

S. Jocelyn Burnell, *Broken for Life* (Swarthmore Lecture), Quaker Home Service, 1989

Jocelyn Burnell's Swarthmore lecture brings her personal and professional experience together with her Quaker belief. The ideas she explores are still current in much Quaker theological thought.

Ben Pink Dandelion, *Open for Transformation: Being Quaker* (Swarthmore Lecture), Quaker Books, 2014

Ben Pink Dandelion's lecture asks what it means to be a Quaker today. This lecture has been widely used as a study resource, prompting Quakers to discuss the issues of conformity and individuality in relation to both practice and belief. It is also available as a video at https://www.youtube.com/watch?v=oRO-lGD9emM

'The Armchair Theologian', a blog by Ben Wood, https://summeroflove85.wordpress.com/

Ben Wood typically writes long posts which bring together his academic theological work, Quakerism, and Anglican background. His main focus is political theology but he has also written about Quaker understandings of the nature of God.

Answering that of God, Peter Parr, The Kindlers, 2012 and *Journeying the Heartlands: Exploring Spiritual Practices of Quaker Worship*, The Kindlers, 2009

The Kindlers are a group who aim to rekindle Quaker spirituality among British meetings. They have published a wide variety of books, all worth reading, of which I have picked out these two as especially relevant because they include material on understandings of God.

Honest to God, John Robinson, SCM Press, 1963

This short book was both controversial and influential when it was first published. Although some of the points have aged, it is still a clear and accessible introduction to some of the central ideas in debates about how we understand God.

Ordinary Theology: Looking, Listening and Learning in Theology, Jeff Astley, Ashgate Publishing Limited, 2002

The approach to doing theology I describe in this book owes a good deal to the work of Jeff Astley. If you would like to explore this approach further, or hear about how it applies outside the Quaker context, *Ordinary Theology* is a good introduction.

Feminist Theology, Natalie Watson, Wm. B. Eerdmans Publishing, 2003

This is an introduction to feminist views in Christianity, which helps readers understand why feminism is important and how it can be helpful to churches. It also contains an annotated bibliography for those who want to go further.

The Nature of Doctrine: Religion and Theology in a Postliberal Age, George Lindbeck, SPCK, 1984

Although I don't discuss it in detail in this book, my thinking has been profoundly influenced by the work of George Lindbeck. In particular, he creates from various sources, including the philosophy of Ludwig Wittgenstein and movements in the sociology of religion, an understanding of what religion is which underpins a number of the ideas I put forward.

The Edge of Words: God and the Habits of Language, Rowan Williams, Bloomsbury Continuum, 2014

Many writers outside the Quaker context have explored these topics, and I have picked this book by Rowan Williams as one which is both clear – not easy to read but not complicated purely for the sake of complication – and erudite. His wide range of sources and discussion partners means that this book would provide an introduction to the broader conversation for a reader who wanted to follow these questions into the more technical areas of theology.

The Quaker Way
A Rediscovery
Rex Ambler
Although fairly well known, Quakerism is not well understood.
The purpose of this book is to explain how Quakerism works as
a spiritual practice.
Paperback: 978-1-78099-657-8 ebook: 978-1-78099-658-5

Blue Sky God
The Evolution of Science and Christianity
Don MacGregor
Quantum consciousness, morphic fields and blue-sky
thinking about God and Jesus the Christ.
Paperback: 978-1-84694-937-1 ebook: 978-1-84694-938-8

Celtic Wheel of the Year
Tess Ward
An original and inspiring selection of prayers combining
Christian and Celtic Pagan traditions, and interweaving their
calendars into a single pattern of prayer for every morning
and night of the year.
Paperback: 978-1-90504-795-6

Christian Atheist
Belonging without Believing
Brian Mountford
Christian Atheists don't believe in God but miss him: especially
the transcendent beauty of his music, language, ethics, and
community.
Paperback: 978-1-84694-439-0 ebook: 978-1-84694-929-6

Compassion Or Apocalypse?
A Comprehensible Guide to the Thoughts of René Girard
James Warren
How René Girard changes the way we think about God and the
Bible, and its relevance for our apocalypse-threatened world.
Paperback: 978-1-78279-073-0 ebook: 978-1-78279-072-3

Diary Of A Gay Priest
The Tightrope Walker
Rev. Dr. Malcolm Johnson
Full of anecdotes and amusing stories, but the Church is still a
dangerous place for a gay priest.
Paperback: 978-1-78279-002-0 ebook: 978-1-78099-999-9

Do You Need God?
Exploring Different Paths to Spirituality Even For Atheists
Rory J.Q. Barnes
An unbiased guide to the building blocks of spiritual belief.
Paperback: 978-1-78279-380-9 ebook: 978-1-78279-379-3

Readers of ebooks can buy or view any of these bestsellers by
clicking on the live link in the title. Most titles are published
in paperback and as an ebook. Paperbacks are available in
traditional bookshops. Both print and ebook formats are
available online.

Find more titles and sign up to our readers' newsletter at
http://www.johnhuntpublishing.com/christianity
Follow us on Facebook at
https://www.facebook.com/ChristianAlternative